Getting Started

What is Tunisian Crochet and how is it different from regular crochet and from knitting?

Tunisian Crochet

Crochet

Knit

Tunisian Crochet, which can also be referred to as an afghan stitch, has a different look than either knitting of regular crochet. To the left are some examples of the very basic stitches of each one.

All three crafts can have much more complicated stitch patterns, of course, but all three are basically just a series of loops created by pulling the yarn through other loops. Some people feel that Tunisian crochet patterns work up faster than the other two, but it really depends on how comfortable you get with working the stitches. When pulling the yarn through the loops, many people find crochet easier because you have a hook and you do not need to "yarn over" in the same way as you do with knitting. Instead of taking your left hand (if you are right-handed) and moving the yarn, you can simply use the hook to wrap around the yarn and pull it through. Many crochet patterns use the term "yarn over" but you can just grab the yarn with your hook instead.

Tunisian crochet can be described as a combination of both knitting and regular crochet. In fact, some stitches, such as the Tunisian Knit Stitch, are extremely similar in looks to knitting stitches, such as the Stockinette Stitch. When knitting, you have a purl stitch which is very similar to the purl stitch in Tunisian crochet. Even though you are using one hook, you keep all the loops on the hook in a similar manner of keeping the loops on your knitting needles.

Unlike regular crochet, Tunisian crochet is worked from side to side and the work is not turned. In Tunisian patterns, you will be given a set of "forward" directions (working right to left across the work) and then a set of "return" directions (working from left to right). The loops are not "pulled through" like in regular crochet – they are kept on the hook during the forward part of each row. Therefore, a long hook with some type of a "stopper" on the end is needed so that the loops can all stay on the hook and not fall off the end. Below is a photo of a Tunisian/Afghan Crochet hook:

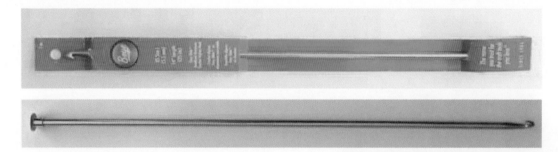

To the right is a photo of regular crochet hooks. They are shorter, without a stopper. At the end of each completed crochet stitch, you only have one loop left on your hook.

On the next page is a photo of knitting needles – they, too, have a stopper on the end, but no hook on the front. In knitting, you need two needles, but with Tunisian crochet, only one hook is used.

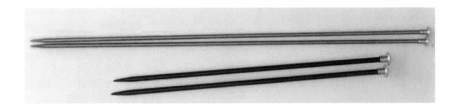

Tunisian crochet forms a tighter fabric than either regular crochet or knitting. Many "regular" crocheters tend to work too tightly when trying out Tunisian crochet. Therefore, a larger than usual hook can be used. In addition, your fabric may curl up when working Tunisian crochet and you may need to straighten out your stitches when you are finished. You can do this by wetting and stretching the fabric, otherwise known as "blocking."

Right & Wrong Sides

For each row, the pattern will give directions for the Forward (Fwd) stitches, going from right to left, and the Return (Rtn) stitches, going from left to right. The right side of the work is always facing up, or towards you. Unlike regular crochet, which can often have a double-sided look, Tunisian crochet will have a Right side (RS) and a Wrong side (WS). In sewing and crafting, we use the term "right" side to refer to the pretty front side of the project, and "wrong" side to refer to the back of the project. I will show photos of both sides for each of the basic stitches.

Choosing a Hook and Yarn

I recommend using a medium worsted weight #4 yarn for your first pattern. A thinner or lighter yarn is slightly harder to work with because the stitches are smaller and harder to see and it can be more difficult to adjust your tension so that your stitches are "even." Most novelty-type yarns are also harder to work with and make it difficult to see the individual stitches. Bulky or chunky yarns might be a good alternative but you will have to use a larger hook. If you use a thick yarn and large hook, your potholders will turn out too large. However, the patterns can easily be adjusted to make larger items, such as baby blankets, afghans, or scarves. Another reason many beginners like to start with a medium worsted yarn is because they are typically easy to find at your local stores and are most often affordably priced.

How do you determine the weight/size of the yarn? Look at the yarn package and you will see one of these following symbols:

1	1 or Super Fine	*(sock, baby and fingering yarn)*
2	2 or Fine	*(baby and sport yarn)*
3	3 or Light	*(light worsted and DK yarn)*
4	4 or Medium	*(worsted, afghan and Aran yarn)*
5	5 or Bulky	*(chunky, craft and rug yarn)*
6	6 or Super Bulky	*(roving and bulky yarn)*

Next to the yarn symbol, you will often see a recommended hook size. When picking out a hook for Tunisian crochet, I would suggest using a larger hook than is recommended. However, since you want a pretty thick potholder (so you don't burn your hands!) you can use the recommended hook. For medium weight yarn, a size I/5.50 mm hook is a good choice.

Holding Your Hook and Adjusting Tension

There are different ways of holding a crochet hook. The pictures in the pattern show how I like to hold it, but you may need to adjust to figure out what is most comfortable for you. For me, the left hand stays steady, and the left index finger adjusts the tension of the yarn coming in. The hook is held close to the front end with the right hand and the right index finger helps to steady the loops on the hook.

Gauge

When making potholders, there is no need to worry much about gauge. Gauge simply refers to how tightly or loosely you work your stitches, which affects the finished size of the project. When you are a beginner, it is more important to just try to make your stitches even. For the example potholders, worked with a size I/5.50 mm hook and #4 medium weight yarn, there are 6 Tss stitches every 2" and 5 Tss rows equal 2". Your potholders might vary in size slightly, but all you really need to worry about is having the back swatch match up in size to the front swatch.

Basic Stitches

This section will teach you the following stitches: The Tunisian Simple Stitch (Tss), The Tunisian Extended Stitch, Tunisian Double Crochet, Tunisian Knit Stitch (Tks), Dropped Stitch, and The Tunisian Purl Stitch (Tps).

To begin working any of the stitches, you will need to make a long length of chain. First, you will make a slip knot. To do this, make a loop (photo 1), fold over and insert hook (photo 2), and pull tight (photo 3):

Next, you will use your hook to pull the yarn through, making a chain. To do this, yarn over (yo) hook (photo 1), pull through (photo 2), continue yo and pull through until you have a length of chain (photo 3).

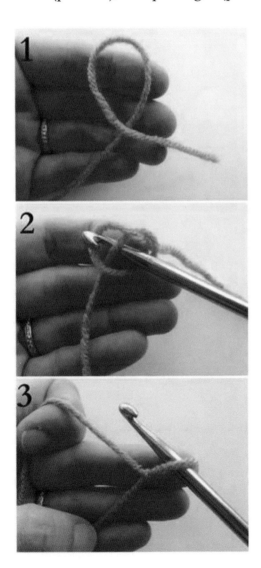

All crochet patterns will tell you how many chains (ch) to start with. Each loop is measured as one chain. When you are making your chains, make sure not to make them too tightly.

Tunisian Simple Stitch (Tss)

The Tunisian Simple Stitch (abbreviated Tss) is the basic "afghan" stitch and many of the other stitches are worked in a similar manner. In fact, almost all the potholder patterns start out with a row of Tss To begin the Tss, you will first make a length of chain (the pattern will tell you how many chains)..

This is how the Tss pattern will read (explanation to follow):

Row 1 - Fwd: Pull up lp in 2nd ch from hook and each ch across. Rtn: yo, pull through 1 lp on hook, *yo, pull through 2 lps on hook* repeat from * to * to end.

Row 2 – Fwd: (lp on hook counts as 1st st). Tss across row. Rtn: yo, pull through 1 lp on hook, *yo, pull through 2 lps on hook* repeat from * to * to end.

Notice how each row has forward (Fwd) directions, and return (Rtn) directions.

Refer to the photos on the following page as you work the first row.

To work the first row, insert your hook in the 2nd chain from hook (photo 1). This is because the first loop actually counts as a stitch and you will always start your rows in the 2nd "stitch". Use your hook to grab the yarn, which is the "yo" or "yarn over" and pull up a loop (photo 2).

Keep working across, inserting your hook into the next chain and pulling up a loop (photo 3) until you get to the end. As you work the loops, you can use your right index finger to steady the loops on the hook and make sure you have the correct tension so that all your loops, and therefore stitches, are even. The next photo shows 22 chains on hook, which is counted as 22 stitches. This is the completed "Fwd" directions of row 1.

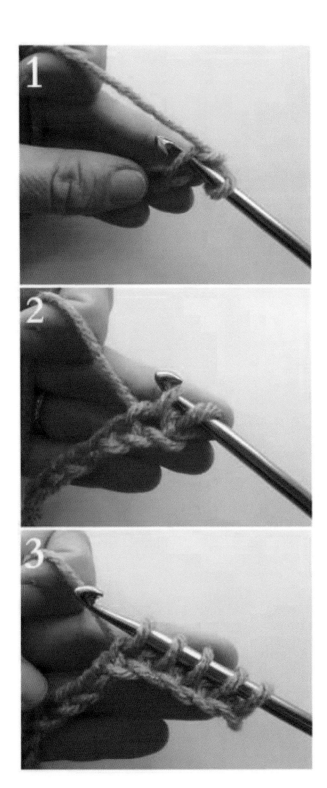

Now, you are ready to work the return. Use your hook to grab the yarn and pull through 1 loop (photo below).

Then, pull through 2 loops at a time. Continue (photo below) until the end.

Row 1 Rtn complete:

Now you are ready to start row 2. Remember, the loop you have left on the hook will always count as the first stitch. So, insert your hook behind the next vertical bar (photo 1) and pull up a loop (photo 2). Continue across (photo 3). This is the Tss.

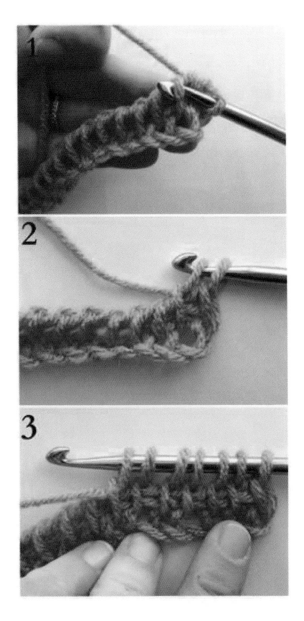

The photo below shows row 2 fwd complete:

Now you can repeat the same thing you did earlier for the return. Simply yo, pull through the first loop, and then pull through two loops at a time to the end.

Now, all you will need to do is repeat what you did in row 2 to complete additional rows of Tss. You will work through the front vertical bar, pulling up loops all the way across. Remember to start with the second vertical bar because the starting loop on your hook counts as a stitch.

The photo to the right shows a back view of completed Tss:

Tunisian Extended Stitch

This stitch is slightly more spread out than the Simple Stitch because you will be adding a "chain 1" to each pull through. Notice how the rtn is the same as the rtn for the Tss.

This is how a row of the Extended Stitch pattern reads: ch 1, *tss in next st, ch 1* repeat from * to * across. Rtn: yo, pull through 1 lp on hook, *yo, pull through 2 lps on hook* repeat from * to * to end.

To begin, you will need to "chain 1". Simply take your hook and pull the yarn through. You do not need to do this as loosely as your starting chain. Next, insert your hook into the next stitch, behind the vertical bar, pull through, and chain 1 again. Repeat this across.

The photo below shows the first few stitches on top of a row of Tss:

Work your return the same as before:

The photo below shows a close up view of the side edge.

The photo below shows the back view of the extended stitch:

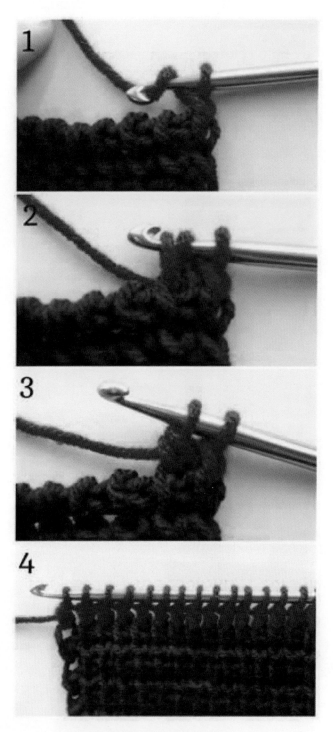

The Tunisian Double Crochet (Tdc) is similar to the Double Crochet in the classic/regular crochet.

To complete this stitch, wrap the yarn around the hook first (photo 1), then insert your hook behind the vertical bar of the next stitch (photo 2), and pull up a loop. Next, pull through 2 loops on hook (photo 3). Repeat across (photo 4).

The pattern directions will often just say "Tdc across" instead of giving details. The rtn is the same as the Tss return.

Photo below shows return row complete:

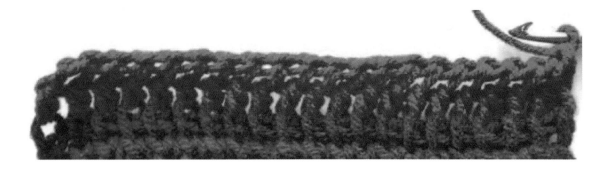

The photo below shows the back view of the Tdc stitch:

Tunisian Knit Stitch (Tks)

This stitch is similar to the Tss, but by simply switching where you insert your hook, the final product has a completely different look. It can naturally be a little tighter than the other stitches, so make sure you do not work it too tightly.

For the Tks, insert your hook **between** the vertical bars, and **under** the horizontal bars:

Pattern directions will often just say "Tks across" instead of giving details. The rtn is the same as the Tss return. Photo shows the completed rtn:

The photo below shows the back view of the Tks stitch:

Dropped Simple Stitch

This is a pretty stitch that works under the horizontal bars instead of through the vertical bars.

To begin to work the dropped stitch pattern, you will need to start with a row of the Tss stitch.

Make sure you do not add or subtract any stitches as you work the rows. To make sure you have the same amount of loops at the end of each fwd row, you will skip a stitch "hole" at the beginning of every fwd even row, and skip a stitch "hole" at the end of each fwd odd row. Also, you will always end each fwd row with a Tss.

Here is how the pattern reads:

"Row 1 – Fwd: Tss across row. Rtn: yo, pull through 1 lp on hook, *yo, pull through 2 lps on hook* repeat from * to * to end.

Row 2 - Fwd: insert hook btwn 2nd and 3rd sts (under the horizontal bars) and pull up a lp, *insert hook btwn next 2 sts and pull up a loop* repeat from * to * across to last st, Tss in last st. Rtn as before.

Row 3 - Fwd: insert hook btwn 1st and 2nd sts (under the horizontal bars) and pull up a lp, *insert hook btwn next 2 sts and pull up a loop* repeat from * to * across to last 2 sts, skip 2nd to last st, Tss in last st. Rtn as before.

Repeat rows 2 and 3 for pattern."

Photos below show start of dropped stitch row:

Photo below shows end of dropped stitch row - fwd:

Photo below shows start of next row:

The photo below shows a back view of the dropped stitch:

Tunisian Purl Stitch (Tps)

This stitch is similar to the purl stitch in knitting. I like to think of it as a backwards Tss.

To make the Tps, move your yarn to the **front** of the work, insert your hook behind the vertical bar, yo and pull up a lp. Rtn is the same as for the Tss (yo, pull through 1 lp on hook, *yo, pull through 2 lps on hook* repeat from * to * to end).

The photos below show the Tps worked on top of a row of Tss.

Move yarn to front of work (photo 1), Insert your hook behind the vertical bar, keeping yarn in front (photo 2), grab the yarn and pull up a lp (photo 3). I like to keep the hook turned up the whole time, and I don't turn the hook at all when working the Fwd row of Tps.

Photo 4 shows 2 full rows of the Tps completed.

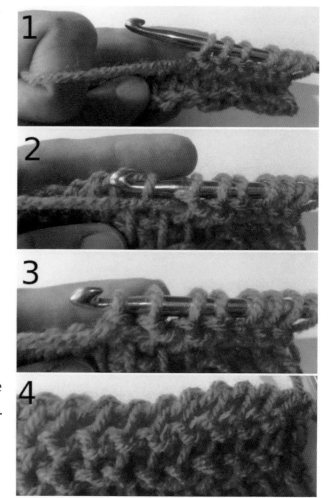

The photo below shows alternating rows of Tss and Tps so you can see the difference between the two.

The photo below shows a back view of Tps:

Introduction & Pattern Notes

Materials:

All 6 patterns can be made with any weight yarn and any size hook, however I would recommend a medium/worsted weight yarn and a size I/5.5mm, J/6.0mm or K/6.5mm hook. This will make a square from about 8" by 8" to 9" by 9", a great size for potholders. Less than 100 yds of yarn is required in total for each potholder.

Abbreviation list:

St(s): stitch(es)

Lp(s): loop(s)

Fwd: forward

Rtn: return

Yo: yarn over

Rep: repeat

Btwn: between

Tss: Tunisian Simple Stitch

Tks: Tunisian Knit Stitch

Tdc: Tunisian Double Crochet

Tps: Tunisian Purl Stitch

Ch: chain

Sl st: Slip stitch

Sc: Single crochet

* * : directions between * and * are meant to be repeated

Note: Many crochet patterns use the term "yarn over" but I often omit this because you can just grab the yarn with your hook and pull through (technically a yo).

Assembly:

All 6 potholders are constructed in a similar manner. A front piece and a back piece are each worked separately, and then joined together with a single crochet (sc) stitch which is a "regular" crochet stitch. To work this final border round, you can either use your Tunisian hook or a regular size I/5.5mm crochet hook. All of the patterns are worked in a similar manner, so you can refer back these photos for help if needed.

Here are the steps to work a single crochet (sc) through both layers to join the potholder edges:

Bring in a new strand of yarn, connecting through both layers with a chain (photo 1). Insert your hook through both layers at once (photo 2). Pull up a loop (photo 3). Pull through both loops on hook (photo 4). Photo 5 shows the border round in progress. To work around the corners, simply work 3 sc stitches into each corner stitch (photo 6). Photo 7 shows the completed border, front view. Photo 8 shows completed border, back view.

To finish off the border round, join to the first stitch in the round with a slip stitch. To do this, insert your hook into the first st and pull the yarn back through the loop on your hook. Then, you are ready to make a length of chain to form the potholder loop (to hang up your potholder). To do this, chain about 10-15 (photo 9), then slip stitch to the potholder border. Tie off (photo 10). To tie off your yarn, simply cut the yarn then work a chain and pull the yarn all the way through – it will tighten into a knot.

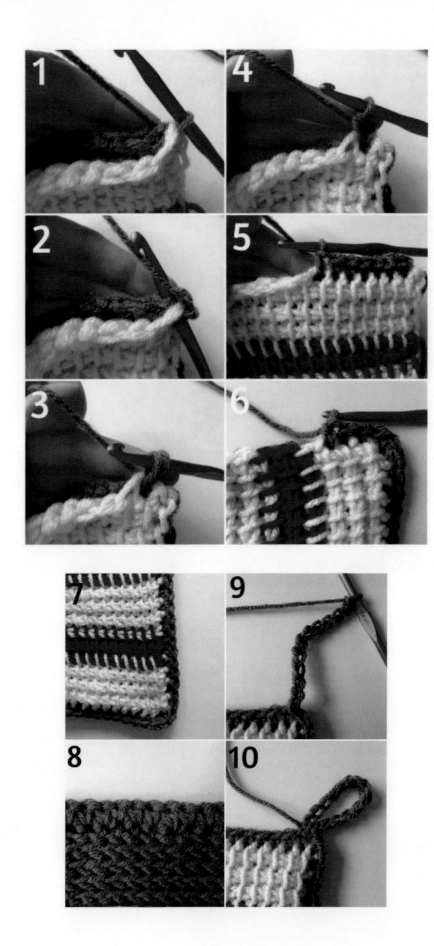

To give your potholder a finished look, use a yarn needle and weave in all the loose ends when you are finished, hiding them between the two layers. It is also possible to work your yarn tail ends into your stitches as you go. However, this can be tricky to figure out, especially when you are just beginning to learn to crochet so I recommend using a needle after you are done.

6 Potholder Patterns

#1 Holiday Inspired Stripes

Example Yarn: Red Heart Super Saver in Burgundy (red), Aran (white) and Hunter Green (green).

Rtn directions for all pattern rows: pull through one loop, *pull through 2 lps* repeated across, until 1 lp remains on hook.

Front piece:

With white, ch 22.

Row 1: Fwd: pull up a loop in 2nd ch from hook and each ch across. Rtn.

Rows 2 and 3: Fwd: Tss in each st across. Rtn.

Row 4: Fwd: Tss in each sst across. At the end of the row 4 forward pass, change to red, keeping white attached for later use. Work the row 4 Rtn with red.

Rows 5: with red, Fwd: Tss in each st across. Rtn.

Row 6: Fwd: Tss in each st across. Change to white at the end of the fwd pass. Rtn as before, but with white.

Rows 7-9: with white, Fwd: Tss in each st across. Rtn.

Row 10: Fwd: Tss in each st across. Change to red at the end of the fwd pass. Rtn as before, but with red.

Rows 11: with red, Fwd: Tss in each st across. Rtn.

Row 12: Fwd: Tss in each st across. Change to white at the end of the fwd pass. Rtn as before, but with white.

Rows 13 – 16: with white, Fwd: Tss in each st across. Rtn.

Row 17: *Tss in next st and pull through lp on hook (1 lp left on hk)* repeated across. Tie off white at the end of row 17.

Back piece:

With green, ch 22.

Row 1: Fwd: pull up a loop in 2nd ch from hook and each ch across. Rtn.

Rows 2 - 21: Fwd: (the lp on the hook counts as the first st) Tks in each st across. Rtn.

Row 22: *Tks in next st and pull through lp on hook (1 lp left on hk)* repeated across. Do not tie off green. Line up front and back pieces with wrong sides together. Then, with green, work the border round in single crochet according to the directions in the "Introduction & Pattern Notes" section.

#2 Basketweave & Ridges

Example Yarn: Red Heart Super Saver in Carrot (orange) and Charcoal (grey).

Rtn directions for all pattern rows: pull through one loop, *pull through 2 lps* repeated across, until 1 lp remains on hook.

Front piece:

With orange, ch 22.

Row 1: Fwd: pull up a loop in 2nd ch from hook and each ch across. Rtn.

Rows 2 - 6: Fwd: (lp on hk counts as first st) Tks in 2nd st and next 4 sts, Tps in next 5 sts, Tks in next 5 sts, Tps in next 5 sts, Tss in last st. Rtn.

Rows 7- 11: Fwd: (lp on hk counts as first st) Tps in 2nd st and next 4 sts, Tks in next 5 sts, Tps in next 5 sts, Tks in next 5 sts, Tss in last st. Rtn.

Rows 12 – 16: repeat rows 2 – 6.

Rows 17 – 20: repeat rows 7 -10.

Row 21: (lp on hk counts as first st) Tps in 2nd st and pull all the way through lp on hook, Tps and pull all the way through in next 4 sts, (Tks and pull all the way through lp on hook) in next 5 sts, (Tps and pull all the way through lp on hook) in next 5 sts, (Tks and pull all the way through lp on hook) in next 5 sts, Tss and pull through lp on hook in last st. Tie off orange.

Back piece:

With grey, ch 22.

Row 1: Fwd: pull up a loop in 2nd ch from hook and each ch across. Rtn.

Rows 2 -4: Fwd: Tss in each st across. Rtn.

Rows 5 -6: Fwd: Tps in each st across. Rtn.

Rows 7-10: Fwd: Tss in each st across. Rtn.

Rows 11-12: Fwd: Tps in each st across. Rtn.

Rows 13 – 16: Fwd: Tss in each st across. Rtn.

Rows 17 -18: Fwd: Tps in each st across. Rtn.

Rows 19 -21: Fwd: Tss in each st across. Rtn.

Row 22: *Tss in next st and pull through lp on hook* repeated across. Do not tie off grey. Line up front and back pieces with wrong sides together. Then, with grey, work the border round in single crochet according to the directions in the "Introduction & Pattern Notes" section.

#3 Colorful Drop Stitch

Example Yarn: **Red Heart Super Saver in White, Aruba Sea (green), Orchid (purple), Lemon (yellow), and Charcoal (grey).**

Rtn directions for all pattern rows: pull through one loop, *pull through 2 lps* repeated across, until 1 lp remains on hook.

To make sure you don't accidentally add or subtract a st in this pattern, make sure you have 22 lps on the hook at the end of each Fwd pass.

Front piece:

With yellow, ch 22.

Row 1: Fwd: pull up a loop in 2nd ch from hook and each ch across. Rtn. Change to purple at the end of row 1.

To change colors, bring the new color in as the last pull through of the last stitch of the rtn row you are finishing. To the right is a photo showing a correct color change:

Row 2: Fwd: with purple, insert hook btwn 2nd and 3rd sts (under the horizontal bars) and pull up a lp, *insert hook btwn next 2 sts (under the horizontal bars) and pull up a loop* repeat from * to * across to last st, Tss in last st. Rtn. Change to green at the end of row 2.

Row 3: Fwd: with green, insert hook btwn 1st and 2nd sts (under the horizontal bars) and pull up a lp, *insert hook btwn next 2 sts (under the horizontal bars) and pull up a loop* repeat from * to * across to last 2 sts, skip 2nd to last st, Tss in last st. Rtn. Change to white at the end of row 3.

Row 4: with white, repeat row 2.

Rows 5-21: All odd rows are the same as row 3. All even rows are the same as row 2. Repeat the color pattern (yellow/purple/green/white), switching each row, until you have reached a total of 21 rows.

Row 22: *insert hook btwn next 2 sts (under the horizontal bars), pull up a lp and through lp on hook (1 lp left on hk)* repeated across. Tss in last st and pull through lp on hook. Tie off.

Back piece:

With grey, ch 22.

Repeat instructions for front side, using all grey. At the end of row 22, do not tie off grey. Line up front and back pieces with wrong sides together. Then, with grey, work the border round in single crochet according to the directions in the "Introduction & Pattern Notes" section.

#4 Lacy White & Blue

Example Yarn: Red Heart Super Saver in White and Periwinkle (blue).

Front piece:

With white, Ch 24.

Row 1: Fwd: pull up a lp in 2nd ch from hook and each ch across. Rtn: pull through 2 lps, *ch 4, pull through 5 lps* repeated across until 3 lps left on hook, ch 3, pull through all 3 lps (photo 1).

Row 2: Fwd: ch 1, pull up lp in each of next 3 ch sts, and pull up lp in each ch of ch-4 loops across (photo 2). (24 sts on hook at the end of row 2 fwd) Rtn: pull through 2 lps, *ch 4, pull through 5 lps* repeated across until 3 lps left on hook, ch 3, pull through all 3 lps.

Rows 3 - 10: repeat row 2. Tie off white at the end of row 10.

Back piece:

Rtn directions for back piece: pull through one loop, *pull through 2 lps* repeated across, until 1 lp remains on hook.

With blue, ch 22.

Row 1: Fwd: pull up a loop in 2nd ch from hook and each ch across. Rtn.

Rows 2 - 22: Fwd: (the lp on the hook counts as the first st) Tks in each st across. Rtn. At the end of row 22, do not tie off blue. Line up front and back pieces with wrong sides together. Then, with blue, work the border round in single crochet according to the directions in the "Introduction & Pattern Notes" section.

#5 Yellow Bobbles

Example Yarn: Peaches N Crème cotton yarn in Sunshine (yellow) and Happy Go Lucky (multicolor).

Special stitch: 3dc cluster: (wrap yarn around hook, insert hook behind vertical bar and pull up a lp, pull through 2 lps) repeated a total of 3 times (photo 1). Yo and pull through 3 lps on hook (photo 2). Photo 3 shows front pattern in progress. 21 lps remain on hook at th end of each Fwd pass.

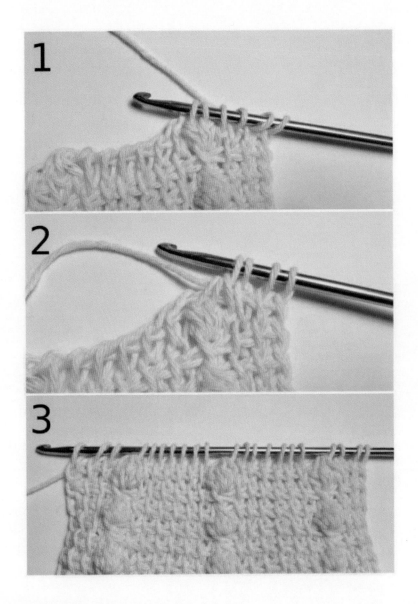

Rtn directions for all pattern rows: pull through one loop, *pull through 2 lps* repeated across, until 1 lp remains on hook.

Front Piece:

With yellow, ch 21.

Row 1: Fwd: pull up a loop in 2nd ch from hook and each ch across. Rtn.

Row 2: Fwd: Tss in first 3 sts (*includes* lp on hook), 3 dc cluster in next st, Tss in next 6 sts, 3 dc cluster, Tss in next 6 sts, 3dc cluster, Tss in last 3 sts. See photo below.

Rtn.

Row 3: Tss in each st across. Rtn.

Rows 4 - 14: for all even rows, repeat row 2. For all odd rows, repeat row 3.

Row 15: *Tss in next st and pull through lp on hook (1 lp left on hk)* repeated across. Tie off yellow at the end of row 15.

Back piece:

With multicolor yarn, ch 21.

Row 1: Fwd: pull up a loop in 2nd ch from hook and each ch across. Rtn.

Rows 2-14: Tss in each st across. Rtn.

Row 15: *Tss in next st and pull through lp on hook (1 lp left on hk)* repeated across.

Do not tie off multicolor yarn. Line up front and back pieces with wrong sides together. Then, with multicolor, work the border round in single crochet according to the directions in the "Introduction & Pattern Notes" section.

Example Yarn: Red Heart Super Saver in Pale Yellow (yellow) and Tea Leaf (green).

Front piece:

For front piece, Rtn: *ch 1, pull through 2 lps* rep across, until 1 lp is left on hk.

With yellow, ch 22.

Row 1: Fwd: Ch 2, pull up a lp in 4th ch from hook, *ch2, sk 1 ch of base ch, insert hook into next ch and pull up a lp* repeated across (photo 1). Rtn (photo 2).

Row 2: Fwd: *Ch2, Tks in next st* rep across (photo 3). Rtn.

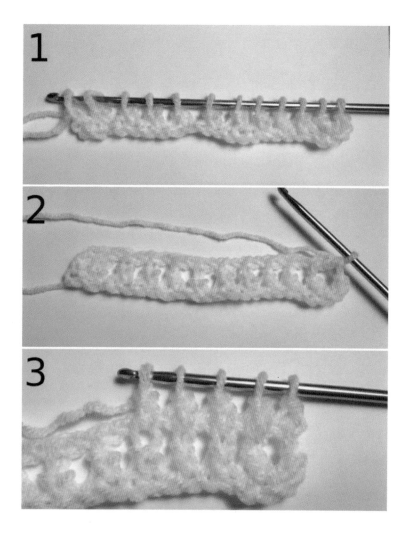

Rows 3 - 9: repeat row 2.

Row 10: *sl st in next ch, Tks in next st and pull all the way through (leaving one lp on hk)* repeated across. Tie off.

Back piece:

Back piece Rtn: pull through one loop, *pull through 2 lps* repeated across, until 1 lp remains on hook.

With green, ch 22.

Row 1: Fwd: pull up a loop in 2nd ch from hook and each ch across. Rtn.

Rows 2-16: *Tss in next st, Tps in next st* rep across, ending with Tss in last st. Rtn.

Row 17: *Tss in next st and pull all the way through (leaving 1 lp on hook), Tps in next st and pull all the way through (leaving 1 lp on hook)* rep across.

Do not tie off green. Line up front and back pieces with wrong sides together. Then, with green, work the border round in single crochet according to the directions in the "Introduction & Pattern Notes" section.

Congratulations!

Projects Complete! You are on your way to becoming a great Tunisian crochet enthusiast and you have a beautiful new set of potholders. You also now know the basics of reading Tunisian crochet patterns!

Printed in Great Britain
by Amazon

25622549R00021